TEN
REASONS

By *Lorin Neikirk*

Also by Lorin Neikirk

Books

"...But That's Another Story!":
My Autistic Insight on Einstein's Brain, Giving Good Blog and Occasional Distractibility

A Little Learning Book About Disrupting Class

A Little Learning Book About Following Directions at School

A Little Learning Book About Sharing

A Little Learning Book About Talking in Class

Jack's Fantastic World Jack's Fantastic World:
(...And The Time He Decided To Paint His Brother's House!)

My Little Social Story About Understanding Autism

Talking, Following Directions, And Disruptions In Class: Three Learning Stories For School

Tools

The Smart Thinkin' line of worksheets and charts

The "Great Idea!" Homework Approach

TEN REASONS

By Lorin Neikirk

Aspie Friendly

www.AspieFriendly.org

ISBN-13: 978-1456448400

ISBN-10: 1456448404

For Addison and Chili

FORWARD

Precisely 2 days ago, I got some bad news.

I had been working on something very important to me for over two years, and when all was said and done, I felt like it didn't turn out the way I really, *really* wanted it to. It was one of those pivotal moments, and I was a more than disappointed with the result.

To console myself about my (self-perceived) failure, I thought of ten reasons to not blame myself for the results. After that, I kept writing lists reflecting positive changes to come from the experience, and other lists to help me adjust to the news.

I was suffering, and although I used the same technique I had used so many times before, this time was a little different. The issue was so enormous to me that while I didn't anticipate that the *Ten Reasons* technique would not work, I was somewhat surprised that it worked as well as it did.

This is a workbook I have intended to write for approximately a year; although I finally understood that that procrastinating any further meant I was doing others a real disservice. People need this technique, just as I needed it two days ago.

The *Ten Reasons* concept is one that I came up with about three years ago, at a time when I had a difficult time understanding the actions I didn't understand of someone I deeply cared for. I was in a relationship with someone, and even though we were "happy", I found that not understanding why he did the things he did was interfering in our relationship, if only because if affected the way I felt about him, or the way I responded to him.

At that time, I was anxious about a very minor thing that he did on occasion. I knew even then that my reaction was without merit, so I thought about some "tragic reasons" he did that thing that was so minor that I shouldn't have given it a second thought. The alternative reasons were those which I would have been 100% fine with, or even evoked a feeling of compassion instead of stress.

It worked so well that I used the same technique in other situations. Thinking of the "Ten Tragic Reasons" helped me be more patient, more tolerant, and it had a huge impact on reducing any stress or anxious feelings.

On other occasions, friends or family would become stressed about the little things in life, and I used the technique to help them see the situation in a new way. A car dodging in and out of traffic could be a real irritation, but imagining that they were on the way to the hospital, because their child was in a car accident, put a new spin on things. Nine more reasons like this, and it was easy to feel compassion for the driver, when others on the road were probably cursing them up and down.

The alternative reasons I used were intentionally dramatic, and although I would try to think of 10 quickly, often relief was found after listing only a few.

The *Ten Reasons* technique is unique, although the concept is based on a principle that is tried-and-true: change the things you can, and let go of the things you can't. The technique, which supports Cognitive Behavioral Therapy efforts of psychologists, is supported by a scientific basis about regarding "retraining" the brain to think differently by redirecting neurological processing. It works for both adults and children, it decreases the need for medications used to alleviate anxiety, and it is inexpensive and easy to do.

In addition to being an effective resource for just about anyone, it is an "Aspie Friendly" technique, meaning it is also useful for those with autism spectrum disorders.

I hope you will enjoy learning about the *Ten Reasons* technique, and that you feel better, every day, as a result!

Lorin Neikirk

AspieFriendly.org

CONTENTS

Section I: Theory and Instructions..............8

Section II: TEN REASONS List Workbook......17

SECTION I: Theory and Instructions

A Scientifically Based Concept and Theory

The *Ten Reasons* technique is one that is supported with a scientific basis with regard to the way the brain processes information, learns to do something new, and is actively "re-trained" to think in a new and healthier way.

The simple explanation about how the brain learns and is "re-trained" is that the more a person thinks a certain way, the easier the brain finds it to think the same way. When a person wants to think differently, it takes work to think in the new way, until the brain finds it as easy or easier to think in the new way.

In a forest, walking repeatedly along a certain route creates a path. Over time, the path becomes even more well-defined, and easier to find and follow. The same path, in the absence of travel, begins to grow over with foliage and becomes more difficult to find and follow. To re-establish the path means traveling the same route until it is again easy to walk along.

The way the brain learns is very similar to a path in a forest. Re-training one's brain is a matter of thinking along a better path often enough, that the path becomes easy for the brain to find and follow.

Neuro-Pathways and Change

When a person "thinks", there are electrical impulses called synapses, which fire in the brain and follow the path to the part of the brain needed to process that information. When a person has a belief, that belief is formed by thinking and re-thinking the belief until the neuro-pathways have traveled the same path often enough that resistance is decreased, making that processing easier. The brain will want to take the path of least resistance when processing information, and if that well-worn path is unhealthy thinking, that will be the path most readily followed by the impulses in the brain.

Changing old thinking into new thinking means working to make the reformed, "new thinking" neuro-pathways those which are less resistant to neurological travel instead. This causes the brain to follow the new thinking as a result.

Belief Systems

Belief systems are not formed overnight. When people feel insecure, it is very often rooted in a belief system which can be traced back a significant amount of time ago. When traumatic events occur, the brain is firing much more than when it is relaxed, creating a neurological environment conducive to reforming new pathways in the heat of the emotional state. This can cause irrational beliefs which feel absolutely warranted. When we have a knee-jerk reaction to a stimulus, that reaction is facilitated by the Amygdule, a part of the brain responsible for instinctual thinking and "fight or flight" responses. When we have a faulty belief system, meaning that it is a belief that is not substantiated, it is a part of our thinking, and that belief system can emerge at times when a speedy response is critical, before the frontal lobe of the brain thinks too much about it. To change our knee-jerk reactions is to change our response. In order to change those knee-jerk reactions, we must change our beliefs.

An important note regarding the *Ten Reasons* technique is that it does not address the reasons a person believes what they do. Whether or not that needs exploration is a decision best made between a person and their mental health professional. The *Ten Reasons* technique does not consider the reason for the belief, as having that immediate relief from anxiety and stress as it is happening can not necessarily be achieved if one must understand the roots of their belief first. Instead of making the individual's belief "accurate", the technique helps the person invalidate the false belief. Additionally, it's not necessary for a person to fully understand their false or irrational belief. The technique operates on the trigger of the specific concern without delving into psychoanalysis.

A refraction of the belief system causes a person's brain to be stimulated in new ways, which takes the neurological travel off the attention of the old belief. In place of the old belief, the person has feelings of compassion, which stimulates that part of the brain. Even if we do not fully understand the reasons why things happen, it is crucial that we approach the incident with positive thinking, and respond to others with an increased level of understanding. These areas are triggered in the brain, making it easier to think this way in the future, irrespective of whether we know the real reason or not.

Ten Reasons Guide

Before one can alleviate bothersome thoughts and/or feelings, the individual must be able to identify that they are happening. At that point, the person asks "What are ten reasons that this could be happening?"

For instance, if the individual has a friend who is occasionally late for get-togethers, that individual may have a belief that the person does not care about the friendship. This may be an irrational belief, as the friend demonstrates other acts of friendship to indicate that they do, in fact, care about the friendship. Although, if the individual's belief system tells them that being tardy means their friend does not care, the belief, or more specifically the individual's response to that belief, is likely to create problems in their interactions.

It has been said that anxiety is worry without good reason. This clearly explains the feeling we can have when we have faulty belief systems that interfere with our interpersonal interactions. We become stressed, anxious, and may even have anxiety or panic attacks. These unfortunate physical symptoms occurring as a result of our beliefs, which may or may not be founded in reality. Understanding the "actual reason" for events which trigger such anxiety is not nearly as important in the *Ten Reasons* method, as realizing that our belief may simply not be accurate. While learning the "actual reason" can be very beneficial, those who are deeply rooted in their faulty belief system can not accept the "actual reason" until they first believe that their own belief may be false. Accepting this is the first step to re-structuring our belief systems and replacing faulty thinking with a healthier perspective.

Listing ten reasons that are tragic in nature distracts and re-trains the brain. If one list brings more thoughts to mind, a new list is created (in addition to the previous list).

The easy steps in the *Ten Reasons* are as follows:

① **Stress/anxiety is self-identified**

② **The event which triggered the anxiety is determined**

③ **The event is listed at the top of a Ten Reasons list worksheet**

④ **Ten logical or compassion-evoking reasons for the trigger are listed**

As a result of following the steps,

the individual's anxiety is reduced to a manageable level

Often, listing the alternate reasons will create the opportunity to explore other anxiety-induced thoughts and beliefs. These new triggers are documented and alternate reasons are listed.

List Example and Explanation

Take for example, that an individual grows up believing that when people are late to meetings, it means that they do not respect the individual they are meeting. As a result, the individual may have very strong feelings about others' ability to be on time. If this individual has a friend who is often late, it will likely causes the individual to question the friendship, and induce a negative reaction when the person is late.

There is a plethora of reasons a person may be late, and if the person is often late to meet any of a number of people or situations, it is a likely that the lack of promptness is rooted in that person's feelings about the other person they are meeting. Although, it is human nature to react to situations based on our belief systems, and a friendship as this one is likely to have some problems. It is each person's prerogative to tolerate another's behavior or not, although faulty beliefs tend to affect not only the one relationship, but many or most of them.

In this example, the individual has a friend who may be chronically late. Although, if the individual's beliefs are very strong, they will also have a negative response to others who are late, regardless of the reason. Often it is only after the negative response is misdirected in such a way as to create a problem for the individual, that the individual begins to question the belief. For instance, if the individual's supervisor at work is detained and is late to a meeting, and the individual makes accusations that the supervisor does not respect the individual, reacting as such is likely to produce a very negative result.

Ten reasons... _why my supervisor was late to our working lunch_

1. _She was talking to HER boss about the raise I asked for._

2. _She got a call from her doctor, and learned her cancer has returned._

3. *She is having a talk with my co-worker, because she learned he has been giving me problems lately.*

4. *She is pregnant and is having morning sickness.*

5. *She was calling other restaurants because she decided last minute we should have steak instead of burgers.*

6. *She was approached by my customer, who wanted to tell her what a wonderful asset I am to the company.*

7. *She got flowers from her husband, who she was afraid didn't love her anymore.*

8. *She ran over a dog on the way, and stopped to find the owner so they can rush the dog to the vet for emergency surgery.*

9. *She just learned her mother is in the hospital and rushed there right away, forgetting entirely about our meeting.*

10. *She ran out of gas on the way here, and her cell phone battery died, and she is walking to a gas station.*

Clearly these alternate reasons are dramatic. Some of the listed reasons may cause the individual to feel compassion (such as #9), and other alternate reasons may cause them to be happy to wait (such as #1).

Depending on the relationship, there may be some animosity, so other alternate reasons may stem from the possibility that the individual may be glad that misfortune fell upon their supervisor (such as #10). Interpersonal relationships are dynamic, so one is able to feel compassion and resentment at the same time. The *Ten Reasons* technique does not judge the alternate reasons, rather encourages the user to find reasons to challenge the thinking which is upsetting.

List-Triggered Lists

As mentioned, listing alternate reasons for the anxiety-trigger may create the opportunity to explore other anxiety-induced thoughts and beliefs.

Belief systems are not isolated, and they are not one-dimensional. If the above individual has a secret fear about a relationship, the #7 reason may trigger some thoughts about their significant other. Let's say the above individual is a man who is afraid his girlfriend may be losing interest in him. Perhaps he gave her flowers and she did not call him to thank him, but instead thanked him the next time she spoke to him on the phone. The man may wonder if this meant she didn't appreciate the flowers, which could prompt a new list.

Indexing

Just one of the great feature of this workbook is the indexing feature. As lists are completed, you have the option to list the topic in an index.

There are two indices which may be referenced when lists are completed. When a list is complete, check the index icon 📖 to indicate that the list will be indexed. At the back of the workbook you can scan the topics and list the page number next to that topic. You can also fill in the blank index section for other topics, or to list a specific list which you believe you will want to quickly reference. On the occasions that anxiety and stress becomes overwhelming, it becomes very easy to re-read lists which have helped with the anxiety in the past.

Section II

The *TEN REASONS* Workbook

Ten reasons why... _____

1 _____
_____

2 _____
_____

3 _____
_____

4 _____
_____

5 _____
_____

6 _____
_____

7 _____
_____

8 _____
_____

9 _____
_____

10 _____
_____

Date_____

Ten reasons why... _____

❶ _____

❷ _____

❸ _____

❹ _____

❺ _____

❻ _____

❼ _____

❽ _____

❾ _____

❿ _____

Date_____

Ten reasons why... _____

❶ _____

_____

❷ _____

_____

❸ _____

_____

❹ _____

_____

❺ _____

_____

❻ _____

_____

❼ _____

_____

❽ _____

_____

❾ _____

_____

❿ _____

_____

Date_____

Ten reasons why... _____

❶ _____

_____

❷ _____

_____

❸ _____

_____

❹ _____

_____

❺ _____

_____

❻ _____

_____

❼ _____

_____

❽ _____

_____

❾ _____

_____

❿ _____

_____

Date_____

Ten reasons why... _____

1 _____

_____

2 _____

_____

3 _____

_____

4 _____

_____

5 _____

_____

6 _____

_____

7 _____

_____

8 _____

_____

9 _____

_____

10 _____

_____

Date_____

Ten reasons why... _____

❶ _____

_____

❷ _____

_____

❸ _____

_____

❹ _____

_____

❺ _____

_____

❻ _____

_____

❼ _____

_____

❽ _____

_____

❾ _____

_____

❿ _____

_____

Date_____

Ten reasons why... _____

1 _____

_____

2 _____

_____

3 _____

_____

4 _____

_____

5 _____

_____

6 _____

_____

7 _____

_____

8 _____

_____

9 _____

_____

10 _____

_____

Date_____

Ten reasons why... _____

❶ _____

_____

❷ _____

_____

❸ _____

_____

❹ _____

_____

❺ _____

_____

❻ _____

_____

❼ _____

_____

❽ _____

_____

❾ _____

_____

❿ _____

_____

Date_____

Ten reasons why... _____

❶ _____
_____

❷ _____
_____

❸ _____
_____

❹ _____
_____

❺ _____
_____

❻ _____
_____

❼ _____
_____

❽ _____
_____

❾ _____
_____

❿ _____
_____

Date_____

Ten reasons why... _____

❶ _____

_____

❷ _____

_____

❸ _____

_____

❹ _____

_____

❺ _____

_____

❻ _____

_____

❼ _____

_____

❽ _____

_____

❾ _____

_____

❿ _____

_____

Date_____

Ten reasons why... _____

1 _____

_____

2 _____

_____

3 _____

_____

4 _____

_____

5 _____

_____

6 _____

_____

7 _____

_____

8 _____

_____

9 _____

_____

10 _____

_____

Date_____

Ten reasons why... _____

❶ _____

_____

❷ _____

_____

❸ _____

_____

❹ _____

_____

❺ _____

_____

❻ _____

_____

❼ _____

_____

❽ _____

_____

❾ _____

_____

❿ _____

_____

Date_____

Ten reasons why... _____

❶ _____

_____

❷ _____

_____

❸ _____

_____

❹ _____

_____

❺ _____

_____

❻ _____

_____

❼ _____

_____

❽ _____

_____

❾ _____

_____

❿ _____

_____

Date_____

Ten reasons why... _____

❶ _____

_____

❷ _____

_____

❸ _____

_____

❹ _____

_____

❺ _____

_____

❻ _____

_____

❼ _____

_____

❽ _____

_____

❾ _____

_____

❿ _____

_____

Date_____

Ten reasons why... _____

❶ _____

_____

❷ _____

_____

❸ _____

_____

❹ _____

_____

❺ _____

_____

❻ _____

_____

❼ _____

_____

❽ _____

_____

❾ _____

_____

❿ _____

_____

Date_____

Ten reasons why... _____

❶ _____

_____

❷ _____

_____

❸ _____

_____

❹ _____

_____

❺ _____

_____

❻ _____

_____

❼ _____

_____

❽ _____

_____

❾ _____

_____

❿ _____

_____

Date_____

Ten reasons why... _____

1 _____
_____

2 _____
_____

3 _____
_____

4 _____
_____

5 _____
_____

6 _____
_____

7 _____
_____

8 _____
_____

9 _____
_____

10 _____
_____

Date_____

Ten reasons why... _____

1 _____
_____

2 _____
_____

3 _____
_____

4 _____
_____

5 _____
_____

6 _____
_____

7 _____
_____

8 _____
_____

9 _____
_____

10 _____
_____

Date_____

Ten reasons why... _____

1 _____
_____

2 _____
_____

3 _____
_____

4 _____
_____

5 _____
_____

6 _____
_____

7 _____
_____

8 _____
_____

9 _____
_____

10 _____
_____

Date_____

Ten reasons why... _____

❶ _____

_____

❷ _____

_____

❸ _____

_____

❹ _____

_____

❺ _____

_____

❻ _____

_____

❼ _____

_____

❽ _____

_____

❾ _____

_____

❿ _____

_____

Date_____

Ten reasons why... _____

❶ _____

_____

❷ _____

_____

❸ _____

_____

❹ _____

_____

❺ _____

_____

❻ _____

_____

❼ _____

_____

❽ _____

_____

❾ _____

_____

❿ _____

_____

Date_____

Ten reasons why... _____

1 _____
_____

2 _____
_____

3 _____
_____

4 _____
_____

5 _____
_____

6 _____
_____

7 _____
_____

8 _____
_____

9 _____
_____

10 _____
_____

Date_____

Ten reasons why... _____

❶ _____

_____

❷ _____

_____

❸ _____

_____

❹ _____

_____

❺ _____

_____

❻ _____

_____

❼ _____

_____

❽ _____

_____

❾ _____

_____

❿ _____

_____

Date_____

Ten reasons why... _____

❶ _____

_____

❷ _____

_____

❸ _____

_____

❹ _____

_____

❺ _____

_____

❻ _____

_____

❼ _____

_____

❽ _____

_____

❾ _____

_____

❿ _____

_____

Date_____

Ten reasons why... _____

① _____

_____

② _____

_____

③ _____

_____

④ _____

_____

⑤ _____

_____

⑥ _____

_____

⑦ _____

_____

⑧ _____

_____

⑨ _____

_____

⑩ _____

_____

Date_____

Ten reasons why... _____

❶ _____

_____

❷ _____

_____

❸ _____

_____

❹ _____

_____

❺ _____

_____

❻ _____

_____

❼ _____

_____

❽ _____

_____

❾ _____

_____

❿ _____

_____

Date_____

Ten reasons why... _____

❶ _____
_____

❷ _____
_____

❸ _____
_____

❹ _____
_____

❺ _____
_____

❻ _____
_____

❼ _____
_____

❽ _____
_____

❾ _____
_____

❿ _____
_____

Date_____

Ten reasons why... _____

1 _____
_____

2 _____
_____

3 _____
_____

4 _____
_____

5 _____
_____

6 _____
_____

7 _____
_____

8 _____
_____

9 _____
_____

10 _____
_____

Date_____

Ten reasons why... _____

1 _____

_____

2 _____

_____

3 _____

_____

4 _____

_____

5 _____

_____

6 _____

_____

7 _____

_____

8 _____

_____

9 _____

_____

10 _____

_____

Date_____

Ten reasons why... _____

1 _____

_____

2 _____

_____

3 _____

_____

4 _____

_____

5 _____

_____

6 _____

_____

7 _____

_____

8 _____

_____

9 _____

_____

10 _____

_____

Date_____

Ten reasons why... _____

1 _____

_____

2 _____

_____

3 _____

_____

4 _____

_____

5 _____

_____

6 _____

_____

7 _____

_____

8 _____

_____

9 _____

_____

10 _____

_____

Date_____

Ten reasons why... _____

❶ _____

_____

❷ _____

_____

❸ _____

_____

❹ _____

_____

❺ _____

_____

❻ _____

_____

❼ _____

_____

❽ _____

_____

❾ _____

_____

❿ _____

_____

Date_____

Ten reasons why... _____

❶ _____

_____

❷ _____

_____

❸ _____

_____

❹ _____

_____

❺ _____

_____

❻ _____

_____

❼ _____

_____

❽ _____

_____

❾ _____

_____

❿ _____

_____

Date_____

Ten reasons why... _____

1 _____
_____

2 _____
_____

3 _____
_____

4 _____
_____

5 _____
_____

6 _____
_____

7 _____
_____

8 _____
_____

9 _____
_____

10 _____
_____

Date_____

Ten reasons why... _____

1 _____

_____

2 _____

_____

3 _____

_____

4 _____

_____

5 _____

_____

6 _____

_____

7 _____

_____

8 _____

_____

9 _____

_____

10 _____

_____

Date_____

Ten reasons why... _____

❶ _____
_____

❷ _____
_____

❸ _____
_____

❹ _____
_____

❺ _____
_____

❻ _____
_____

❼ _____
_____

❽ _____
_____

❾ _____
_____

❿ _____
_____
_____

Date_____

Ten reasons why... _____

1 _____

_____

2 _____

_____

3 _____

_____

4 _____

_____

5 _____

_____

6 _____

_____

7 _____

_____

8 _____

_____

9 _____

_____

10 _____

_____

Date_____

Ten reasons why... _____

❶ _____

_____

❷ _____

_____

❸ _____

_____

❹ _____

_____

❺ _____

_____

❻ _____

_____

❼ _____

_____

❽ _____

_____

❾ _____

_____

❿ _____

_____

Date_____

Ten reasons why... _____

1 _____
_____

2 _____
_____

3 _____
_____

4 _____
_____

5 _____
_____

6 _____
_____

7 _____
_____

8 _____
_____

9 _____
_____

10 _____
_____

Date_____

Ten reasons why... _____

❶ _____
_____

❷ _____
_____

❸ _____
_____

❹ _____
_____

❺ _____
_____

❻ _____
_____

❼ _____
_____

❽ _____
_____

❾ _____
_____

❿ _____
_____

Date_____

Ten reasons why... _____

❶ _____
_____

❷ _____
_____

❸ _____
_____

❹ _____
_____

❺ _____
_____

❻ _____
_____

❼ _____
_____

❽ _____
_____

❾ _____
_____

❿ _____
_____

Date_____

Ten reasons why... _____

❶ _____

_____

❷ _____

_____

❸ _____

_____

❹ _____

_____

❺ _____

_____

❻ _____

_____

❼ _____

_____

❽ _____

_____

❾ _____

_____

❿ _____

_____

_____

Date_____

Ten reasons why... _____

❶ _____

_____

❷ _____

_____

❸ _____

_____

❹ _____

_____

❺ _____

_____

❻ _____

_____

❼ _____

_____

❽ _____

_____

❾ _____

_____

❿ _____

_____

Date_____

Ten reasons why... _____

❶ _____

❷ _____

❸ _____

❹ _____

❺ _____

❻ _____

❼ _____

❽ _____

❾ _____

❿ _____

Date_____

Ten reasons why... _____

❶ _____

_____

❷ _____

_____

❸ _____

_____

❹ _____

_____

❺ _____

_____

❻ _____

_____

❼ _____

_____

❽ _____

_____

❾ _____

_____

❿ _____

_____

Date_____

Ten reasons why... _____

1 _____

_____

2 _____

_____

3 _____

_____

4 _____

_____

5 _____

_____

6 _____

_____

7 _____

_____

8 _____

_____

9 _____

_____

10 _____

_____

Date_____

Ten reasons why... _____

1 _____

_____

2 _____

_____

3 _____

_____

4 _____

_____

5 _____

_____

6 _____

_____

7 _____

_____

8 _____

_____

9 _____

_____

10 _____

_____

Date_____

Ten reasons why... _____

1 _____

_____

2 _____

_____

3 _____

_____

4 _____

_____

5 _____

_____

6 _____

_____

7 _____

_____

8 _____

_____

9 _____

_____

10 _____

_____

Date_____

Ten reasons why... _____

❶ _____

_____

❷ _____

_____

❸ _____

_____

❹ _____

_____

❺ _____

_____

❻ _____

_____

❼ _____

_____

❽ _____

_____

❾ _____

_____

❿ _____

_____

Date_____

Ten reasons why... _____

1 _____

_____

2 _____

_____

3 _____

_____

4 _____

_____

5 _____

_____

6 _____

_____

7 _____

_____

8 _____

_____

9 _____

_____

10 _____

_____

_____

Date_____

Ten reasons why... _____

❶ _____

_____

❷ _____

_____

❸ _____

_____

❹ _____

_____

❺ _____

_____

❻ _____

_____

❼ _____

_____

❽ _____

_____

❾ _____

_____

❿ _____

_____

Date_____

Ten reasons why... _____

❶ _____

_____

❷ _____

_____

❸ _____

_____

❹ _____

_____

❺ _____

_____

❻ _____

_____

❼ _____

_____

❽ _____

_____

❾ _____

_____

❿ _____

_____

Date_____

Ten reasons why... _____

❶ _____

_____

❷ _____

_____

❸ _____

_____

❹ _____

_____

❺ _____

_____

❻ _____

_____

❼ _____

_____

❽ _____

_____

❾ _____

_____

❿ _____

_____

Date_____

Ten reasons why... _____

1 _____

_____

2 _____

_____

3 _____

_____

4 _____

_____

5 _____

_____

6 _____

_____

7 _____

_____

8 _____

_____

9 _____

_____

10 _____

_____

Date_____

Ten reasons why... _____

❶ _____

_____

❷ _____

_____

❸ _____

_____

❹ _____

_____

❺ _____

_____

❻ _____

_____

❼ _____

_____

❽ _____

_____

❾ _____

_____

❿ _____

_____

Date_____

Ten reasons why... _____

❶ _____
_____

❷ _____
_____

❸ _____
_____

❹ _____
_____

❺ _____
_____

❻ _____
_____

❼ _____
_____

❽ _____
_____

❾ _____
_____

❿ _____
_____

Date_____

Ten reasons why... _____

❶ _____
_____

❷ _____
_____

❸ _____
_____

❹ _____
_____

❺ _____
_____

❻ _____
_____

❼ _____
_____

❽ _____
_____

❾ _____
_____

❿ _____
_____

Date_____

Ten reasons why... _____

1 _____

_____

2 _____

_____

3 _____

_____

4 _____

_____

5 _____

_____

6 _____

_____

7 _____

_____

8 _____

_____

9 _____

_____

10 _____

_____

Date_____

Ten reasons why... _____

1 _____

_____

2 _____

_____

3 _____

_____

4 _____

_____

5 _____

_____

6 _____

_____

7 _____

_____

8 _____

_____

9 _____

_____

10 _____

_____

Date_____

Ten reasons why... _____

❶ _____

_____

❷ _____

_____

❸ _____

_____

❹ _____

_____

❺ _____

_____

❻ _____

_____

❼ _____

_____

❽ _____

_____

❾ _____

_____

❿ _____

_____

Date_____

Ten reasons why... _____

1 _____

_____

2 _____

_____

3 _____

_____

4 _____

_____

5 _____

_____

6 _____

_____

7 _____

_____

8 _____

_____

9 _____

_____

10 _____

_____

Date_____

Ten reasons why... _____

❶ _____

_____

❷ _____

_____

❸ _____

_____

❹ _____

_____

❺ _____

_____

❻ _____

_____

❼ _____

_____

❽ _____

_____

❾ _____

_____

❿ _____

_____

Date_____

Ten reasons why... _____

❶ _____
_____

❷ _____
_____

❸ _____
_____

❹ _____
_____

❺ _____
_____

❻ _____
_____

❼ _____
_____

❽ _____
_____

❾ _____
_____

❿ _____
_____

Date_____

Ten reasons why... _____

1 _____

_____

2 _____

_____

3 _____

_____

4 _____

_____

5 _____

_____

6 _____

_____

7 _____

_____

8 _____

_____

9 _____

_____

10 _____

_____

Date_____

Ten reasons why... _____

❶ _____
_____

❷ _____
_____

❸ _____
_____

❹ _____
_____

❺ _____
_____

❻ _____
_____

❼ _____
_____

❽ _____
_____

❾ _____
_____

❿ _____
_____

Date_____

Ten reasons why... _____

1 _____

_____

2 _____

_____

3 _____

_____

4 _____

_____

5 _____

_____

6 _____

_____

7 _____

_____

8 _____

_____

9 _____

_____

10 _____

_____

Date_____

Ten reasons why... _____

1 _____

_____

2 _____

_____

3 _____

_____

4 _____

_____

5 _____

_____

6 _____

_____

7 _____

_____

8 _____

_____

9 _____

_____

10 _____

_____

Date_____

Ten reasons why... _____

❶ _____

_____

❷ _____

_____

❸ _____

_____

❹ _____

_____

❺ _____

_____

❻ _____

_____

❼ _____

_____

❽ _____

_____

❾ _____

_____

❿ _____

_____

Date_____

Ten reasons why... _____

1 _____

_____

2 _____

_____

3 _____

_____

4 _____

_____

5 _____

_____

6 _____

_____

7 _____

_____

8 _____

_____

9 _____

_____

10 _____

_____

Date_____

Ten reasons why... _____

❶ _____
_____

❷ _____
_____

❸ _____
_____

❹ _____
_____

❺ _____
_____

❻ _____
_____

❼ _____
_____

❽ _____
_____

❾ _____
_____

❿ _____
_____

Date_____

Ten reasons why... _____

❶ _____

_____

❷ _____

_____

❸ _____

_____

❹ _____

_____

❺ _____

_____

❻ _____

_____

❼ _____

_____

❽ _____

_____

❾ _____

_____

❿ _____

_____

Date_____

Ten reasons why... _____

❶ _____

❷ _____

❸ _____

❹ _____

❺ _____

❻ _____

❼ _____

❽ _____

❾ _____

❿ _____

Date_____

INDEX
Pre-Defined Subject Index

List Page Numbers:

Dating

Day

Dishonesty

Effort

Envy

Expectations

Father

Food

Friend

Fun

Games

Girlfriend

Going Out

Health

Honesty _____

House _____

Housework _____

_____

_____

_____

Interest _____

_____

_____

Jealousy _____

_____

_____

Kids _____

_____

_____

Listening _____

_____

_____

Miscommunication _____

Money _____

Mother _____

_____

Night

Objective

Party
Pets
Physical Activity
Purchases

Quiet

Relationships

School

Social Events _____

Social Media _____

Spouse _____

Stress _____

_____

_____

_____

Talking _____

Telephone _____

_____

_____

Understanding _____

_____

_____

_____

Violence _____

_____

_____

_____

Weight _____

Work _____

_____

_____

_____

_____

User-Defined Subject Index

Subject   **List Page Numbers:**

_____

_____

_____

_____

_____

_____

_____

_____

_____

_____

_____

_____

_____

_____

_____

_____

_____

_____

_____

_____

About the Author

Lorin Neikirk is an Autism Consultant, author, and founder of Aspie Friendly. Lorin has been writing learning books for students since 2003, and has a line of tools designed for productivity in the classroom.

As an adult with autism, Lorin understands the way the autistic brain processes information, and uses this understanding to help parents of kids with autism, as well as student who are not on the autism spectrum. Neikirk, who resides in Houston, Texas, has gained international attention for her books and productivity tools, as well as attention from organizations, such as Easter Seals, Advancing Futures for Adults with Autism and The Autism Legislation Project.

Neikirk recently founded Autistic Survivors Protecting Ourselves. The non-profit organizations teaches Spectrum Individuals how to identify abusive situations and relationships, and to self-advocate. Much the way children with autism must learn to protect themselves from bullies, and get needed guidance in the interim, ASPO teaches adults with autism the same, in the context of adulthood. For more information please visit www.AspieFriendly.org and www.AS-PO.org.

Autism. Understand it.

Filename: TEN REASONS.doc
Directory: E:\Aspie Friendly\Working Files\Book-TEN REASONS
Template: C:\Documents and Settings\Administrator\Application
    Data\Microsoft\Templates\LuLuPDF69.dot
Title:
Subject:
Author: Craig Lightfoot
Keywords:
Comments:
Creation Date: 12/5/2010 11:21:00 AM
Change Number: 9
Last Saved On: 12/5/2010 7:55:00 PM
Last Saved By: Lorin Neikirk
Total Editing Time: 378 Minutes
Last Printed On: 12/5/2010 7:55:00 PM
As of Last Complete Printing
    Number of Pages: 101
    Number of Words: 3,282 (approx.)
    Number of Characters: 16,412 (approx.)

www.ingramcontent.com/pod-product-compliance
Lightning Source LLC
Chambersburg PA
CBHW062040280526
45788CB00003B/1048